Mixing it up with . . .

The Simpsons

Also available in the same series:

Owen Smith, *Mixing it up with . . . Football*
Owen Smith, *Mixing it up with . . . Harry Potter*

Mixing it up with . . .

The Simpsons

12 sessions about faith for 9–13s

Owen Smith

CHURCH HOUSE
PUBLISHING

Church House Publishing
Church House
Great Smith Street
London SW1P 3AZ
Tel: 020 7898 1451
Fax: 020 7898 1449

ISBN 978-0-7151-4104-5

Published 2007 by Church House Publishing.

Bible quotations are from THE HOLY BIBLE, NEW INTERNATIONAL VERSION,
Copyright © 1973, 1978, 1984 by International Bible Society. Used by permission
of International Bible Society.

The opinions expressed in this book are those of the author and do not
necessarily reflect the official policy of the General Synod of the Archbishops'
Council of the Church of England.

Cover design by www.penquinboy.net
Printed in England by Halstan and Co. Ltd, Amersham, Bucks

Contents

Contents

Introduction

How this book came about

Six months after I started work at St Margaret's Church, Rainham, Kent, I carried out a review of all our activities with young people to identify which groups we were working with and which we were failing to reach. As part of that review, it became clear that there were certain gaps in our work. One such gap was suitable provision for the ten- and eleven-year-old boys, who were too young to come along to the church youth group and either found that the style of the Sunday morning provision we had at the time didn't cater to their interests, or were unable to come at all on Sunday because of football matches and other commitments.

We identified some boys who came from families within the congregation and some who were known to us through outreach projects we had recently run in the local community and invited them to a midweek group, later dubbed 'Superb'. As I looked round for material aimed at the nine to thirteen age group, I found that there was very little available and even less that capitalized on the interests of young people of this age.

With this in mind, I set about writing some material that used examples of the culture in which these young people were immersed to introduce and explore relevant Christian themes. These sessions are the result!

Who is this material for?

A recent study found that more young people stopped coming to church at the age of eleven than at any other age.[1] Yet this is an age group that is largely under-resourced by churches. This material is suitable for young people aged nine to thirteen who already have some church involvement and also for those on the fringe who may find it too difficult to come to other church activities for cultural reasons or because the times of regular church groups are inconvenient.

As the activities do not require a huge amount of space, the material may be used with a midweek group, a Sunday school, or a school lunchtime group. Each session lasts about 45 minutes, but the length can be tailored to suit your individual setting, and extra material is provided should you wish to run a longer session. Forty-five minutes is only long enough to provide an introduction to a topic. If in the course of the sessions, you find that a certain issue or question is of particular interest to your young people, you can go back to it and cover it in greater depth at a later date.

Working with nine- to thirteen-year-olds

Young people between nine and thirteen are undergoing a huge number of changes — both physically and mentally. They are about to embark on the often treacherous journey through adolescence, and are beginning to know their own mind. They are moving away from their parents towards their peers and are developing the sense of self that they'll carry with them into their adult lives.[2] They have a new-found capacity for abstract thought and can now consider a variety of opinions and possible outcomes, thinking through situations without needing concrete experiences.[3] All this means that groups and activities for this age range should differ from those aimed at younger children or teenagers.

Setting up a group

When setting up a group, there are a number of things it's important to consider.

Who is your group aimed at?

First, you will need to decide:
- Is it a group that provides an opportunity for young people with no previous contact with the church to start thinking about some Christian themes?
- Is it a group that seeks to nurture and encourage the young people who are already part of the church community?
- Is it a combination of the two?

You might also want to think about whether your young people will feel more comfortable meeting in a single-sex group. This will depend on the personalities and the gender breakdown of the young people you are aiming at.

When to hold your group

You need to identify the best time for your group to meet. It might be that you will use this material with a group as part of your provision for children and young people on a Sunday morning. You might find, however, as we did, that Sunday is not a good time for nine- to thirteen-year-olds to come to a group such as this since many play sports and have other activities and commitments on Sunday mornings. Thankfully, we are moving away from the idea that church and worship only take place on a Sunday and it may be that your work with this age group needs a 'fresh expression' of church. For more about such groups and initiatives, have a look at the fresh expressions website – www.freshexpressions.org.uk.

Venue

It's also important to have thought through the 'where' of your group. The venue for your sessions is very important in determining how your group will run – the environment can have a huge impact on how a session goes. It may be that you have limited options over where you can meet. But you do need a room free of major distractions and big enough to allow your group to relax in comfort. You will also need a television and a DVD player. Possible venues might include the home of a member of the group, the vicarage (as long as you've asked the vicar first!) or the church hall. Wherever you decide to meet, you must make sure that you are following the child protection guidelines set by your Church or organization – more about this below.

Ground rules

As your group begins to meet, you may find it useful to come up with some kind of agreement about how the group will work. Obviously you don't want the sessions to feel like school, but it's often good to get your young people to come up with a few basic ground rules that set out what is expected of each member, including you, and what behaviour is not acceptable to the group. These rules might include the group's thoughts about how they should treat one another and the place in which you meet. Some rules could also be included to make sure that your group is a 'safe' environment where everyone feels able to contribute to the discussions. Such rules might include keeping within the group the things different people share during sessions rather than talking about them to other friends afterwards, and making sure that everyone gets a chance to say what they think without being interrupted.

Group identity

Establishing a strong group identity and a sense of ownership of the group is essential when working with nines to thirteens. These young people are at a point in their lives when 'belonging' is very important. While being careful not to set up cliques, you need to make your group one to which the young people feel attached. This can be an important part of maintaining their interest, particularly as they make the transition from primary to secondary education. When I started a group, I got the young people to come up with a name during the first session. Introducing regular occurrences unique to the group can also help to bond the young people. These might be simple things like always having doughnuts when it's someone's birthday, having some sort of reward if a group member brings their own Bible to a session, or giving a prize to the first person to find the Bible passage.

Good practice: child protection and health and safety

It's important that you make yourself aware of the guidelines your organization has in place to protect you as a leader and the young people you are working with. These will probably take the form of a child protection policy and good practice guidelines, and will be available from your Diocesan, or your denomination's, Children's or Youth Officer. Making yourself aware of these guidelines is a key part of preparing yourself to run a group. On the basis of these guidelines, you will need to consider how many leaders your group will need to have present when it meets. For young people aged eight and over, the normal ratio is one leader for every eight young people, with a minimum of two leaders.

You will also need to consider what contact information and parental permission you need to seek from the young people who will attend your group. For more information on matters relating to child protection and best practice, get in touch with your Diocesan Youth Officer, or your denomination's equivalent, who will be happy to give you further advice.

Handling sensitive issues

Some of the sessions in this book cover topics that might bring up issues that will be sensitive for particular members of the group. Talking about subjects such as families, or self-image, might raise both positive and negative anxieties, memories and experiences. If a young person shares such feelings, it may be appropriate to talk them through as part of the discussion during the session – young people are often surprisingly mature when it appears that a member of their group is hurting. Sometimes, however, it might be better to suggest gently that you talk to the young person at a more suitable time. Be careful, though, not to diminish the importance of what they have said or want to share. If at any point you feel that you are getting out of your depth – don't keep going! It may be that you need to talk to your vicar or line manager about getting help from someone with more experience in dealing with such issues. You don't have to know all the answers, but knowing where to find out more is a good start!

Encouraging your group to talk

Some of the activities included within the sessions involve discussion and this might prove difficult for some groups. Some young people will feed off one another's ideas and will be able to hold interesting and lively discussions. In such groups, make sure that one or two people aren't monopolizing the discussion. You might need to draw in the quieter members of the group, gently inviting them to contribute, remembering that they might not want to say anything! If the discussion becomes too rowdy, you might need to pause for a moment and make sure that members take turns to contribute their opinions.

When faced with a question for discussion, other groups will sit in silence, avoiding eye contact with anyone in the room. Initially, don't worry about silence – it might just take a moment for the young people to process what you are asking. However, if the silence persists, you may need to restate the question, breaking it down into simpler ideas. Use open questions to stimulate the discussion – questions that can't simply be answered by a 'yes' or a 'no'. Sometimes, it may work better to ask the group to discuss a particular issue from the point of view of a third party within a scenario. Some groups will find it much easier to talk about how 'David' or 'Helen' might feel or act in a certain situation, rather than how they themselves would feel or act.

Why use contemporary culture?

Using the culture of the day to help engage people in thinking about Christian themes is not a new idea! When Jesus taught the people he met on his travels, he used stories and illustrations firmly rooted in the culture of the time. The parables he used to convey his messages had agricultural or social settings with which his audience would have been able to identify.

In the past, the Church has sometimes appeared more wary of the ever-expanding influence that media such as television and film have on people, sometimes perceiving them more as a threat than an aid. Today, young people coming to the end of primary school and starting secondary education are immersed in a culture of satellite TV, Playstations, celebrities, *Big Brother* and footballers. It is a culture where 'anything goes' and 'want it *now*' seem to be the prevailing philosophies. In order to engage with these young people we need to use the heroes and images they encounter daily to explore what are often, to them, unfamiliar Christian themes.

Many aspects of contemporary culture can be used to introduce and explore Christian themes. If the interests of the young people in your group lie more in music than *The Simpsons*, then using lyrics from their favourite songs might be an excellent basis for a session. You might want to look at resources such as *Music to Move the Soul*[4] for examples of such material. *Youthwork Magazine* (www.youthwork.co.uk) has regular features showing how different aspects of youth culture can be used in this way.

The Internet is an amazing tool for developing such sessions – you can find episode summaries, plot synopses, quotations from films and lyrics for songs, as well as a wealth of background material and trivia.

Why use *The Simpsons*?

The Simpsons is a prime example of popular culture that has made its mark on our young people. In a survey of over two thousand ten- to fourteen-year-olds conducted by the Christian Research Association, 11 out of 17 said that their most watched programme was *The Simpsons*.[5] With memorable characters and hilarious storylines, it provides a wealth of material that can be used to introduce and discuss Christian themes. The exploration of real-life issues and even complex theological concepts can be simplified by drawing parallels with situations and incidents in the lives of these well-known cartoon characters. *The Simpsons* is also hugely moral, with many episodes dealing with issues and dilemmas faced by the young people in their own lives. The willingness of the show's writers to deal with questions of both morality and spirituality makes the programme an ideal tool.

This book uses episodes from one season of *The Simpsons* (season 4), so that you only need to purchase or borrow one season's DVD or video. However, you can of course invent your own sessions following the model presented here and using other seasons of *The Simpsons*.

Caution!

Not every episode of *The Simpsons* is suitable to be shown to your youth group. It is possible that there will even be things in the episodes used during these sessions that you might think aren't necessarily to be encouraged in our young people. There will, however, always be elements of popular culture that are not, as Paul said, as good, as pure or as admirable as we would like (Philippians 4.8). It is our responsibility to make it clear to our young people that there are features of the culture in which we live that are good and to be encouraged, and features that we need to be more wary of. As Christians we cannot establish ourselves as islands, detached from the culture that permeates all areas of our lives – Jesus called us to be in the world, but not of it. We need to support our young people as they form their opinions of the world around them, and equip them with the ability to discern those things that are not acceptable. During the sessions you might want to mention some of the less admirable aspects of *The Simpsons* as they arise, challenging the group over their thoughts about them.

The shape of this book

This book contains twelve sessions. Each session is designed to last just under an hour. Different groups, however, will have different lengths of time in which to run their sessions. If your group is pushed for time because, for example, it meets during a lunch-hour, you can run the cut-down session that lasts about forty minutes, limiting yourself to a key clip from the episode. Other groups might have more than an hour to fill, or might get through the activities very quickly. For groups such as these, I've included some extra activities that are not crucial to the point of the session, but are linked to the theme.

The twelve sessions are divided into two groups. The first six sessions are aimed at young people who are just beginning to explore the Christian faith. They cover some of the basic questions that arise when we start to think about what Christians believe.

The second six sessions cover issues that will be relevant and accessible to young people with a slightly greater knowledge of the Bible and of Christianity.

Each session includes a list of everything you will need and 'prompts' for leaders to guide discussion of Bible passages and the prayer times.

The shape of each session

Each session includes the following:

Beforehand . . . This tells the person leading the group about any preparation that will need to be done before the session starts.

Opening activity . . . This activity introduces the session's theme and its purpose is to get the young people thinking about the issue. It is usually quite short, lasting between 5 and 15 minutes.

Simpsons episode . . . This issue is then explored further in an episode of *The Simpsons* (or clips from the episode if your time is limited). There are questions for discussion that draw out the point of the episode. These questions can be discussed either as a whole group, or in smaller groups or pairs or threes who then feed back their ideas to the whole group.

 **Bible focus . . .** The young people look up a Bible verse or passage that deals with the Christian perspective on the session's theme. Here the verses are quoted from the NIV, but you might like to use the version your group members know best.

 Prayer response . . . Each session ends with a prayer activity drawing on the theme and giving the young people a chance to respond in some way.

 **Extras and inserts . . .** These are optional activities that you can choose to include in your session if you think your group will get through the rest of the session very quickly. The activities are linked to the theme, but are not essential to communicating it and can therefore be added at any point.

Thanks

The writing of this book has involved the patience of a lot of people, to all of whom I owe a great deal! I'd like to thank my Superb cell group (Ross, Alex, Tom, Jack, Joe, Connor, Craig, John, David, Fenner and Nick) for helping me refine the sessions and telling me what they thought with no holds barred! I'd like to thank the youth groups and youth workers of St Mary's Church, Tonbridge, the parish of Rochester and Christchurch, Chislehurst, for trying out the sessions and sending me their feedback. Finally, my thanks go to my boss Canon Alan Vousden for enduring my constant mess in his nice clean office and to our wonderful Rochester Diocesan Youth Adviser Phil Greig for making me think about publishing these sessions in the first place.

Notes

1   Peter Brierley, *Reaching and Keeping Tweenagers*, Christian Research Association, 2003.
2   Erik H. Erikson, *Identity: Youth and Crisis*, W. W. Norton, 1968.
3   Jean Piaget (translated by W. Mays), *The Principles of Genetic Epistemology*, Routledge, 1972.
4   Steve and Ruth Adams, *Music to Move the Soul*, Spring Harvest, 2003.
5   Peter Brierley, *Reaching and Keeping Tweenagers*.

PART ONE

Laying foundations

Luvvuuuurve
GOD'S LOVE FOR US

SESSION AIM........ **To think about what it means when we say that God loves us**

EPISODE............ I Love Lisa (season 4, episode 15)

CLIP............... Start the clip just after Homer says, 'Can you believe Flanders threw out a perfectly good toothbrush . . .' (time code: 10:00) and end it just after Bart says, 'And . . . *now* . . .' (Duration: 5:16)

SYNOPSIS........... Lisa's valentine to the most disliked boy in her class causes her to be chased by him

KEY QUOTE.......... **Ralph:** I love Lisa Simpson and when I grow up, I'm going to marry her.

BIBLE FOCUS........ 'This is how God showed his love among us: He sent his one and only Son into the world that we might live through him. This is love: not that we loved God, but that he loved us and sent his Son as an atoning sacrifice for our sins.' (1 John 4.9-10)

RESOURCES.......... *Season 4 DVD 3, Bibles, Love Heart sweets, quiet music for the meditation*

EXTRAS AND INSERTS *Collection of classic and recent love songs, fruit and vegetables, Jammie Dodger biscuits (the biscuit with the heart-shaped hole in the top), one biscuit for every group member*

● Make sure you've taken out any of the Love Hearts that you think are unsuitable for your young people.

I love you, Honey, but I just can't smile
(10 minutes)
Get the young people to sit in a circle and then choose one to stand in the middle. The aim of the game is for the person in the middle to make someone in the circle laugh. They do this by going up to one of those sitting down and saying, 'Honey, if you love me, just smile.' The person has to reply, without laughing or smiling, 'Honey, you know I love you, but I just can't smile.' If at any point they do laugh, they become the one in the middle. If they don't laugh, the player in the middle has to move on to someone else. When all those who would like to be in the middle have had a go, introduce the theme for the session.

on simpsons

I love Lisa
(25 minutes)

Watch the episode, or the clip if time is limited, in which we see Ralph declare his love for Lisa after she gives him a Valentine's Day card. Get the group to think about the following questions:

- How did Ralph demonstrate his love for Lisa? (He tarred the roof of the Simpson's house, gave Lisa presents and bought her tickets to the Krusty show.)
- What had she done to deserve these things? (She'd given him a valentine card.)
- Was Ralph really in love with Lisa? (Not really – he just liked having someone treat him nicely.)

on Bible passage

Love demonstrated
(10 minutes)

The Bible is the amazing account of God's love for his people – from beginning to end we see the different ways in which God shows how much he loves us. John summarizes the major expression of God's love in 1 John 4.9-10.

Get the group to look up the verses and discuss the following questions:

- How did God show that he loves us? (He sent Jesus into the world to die on the cross.)
- What did anyone do to deserve this sacrifice? (Nothing – God acted out of love, not because of anything anyone had done. This is still true. We've done nothing to deserve God's love and forgiveness.)
- What does 'atoning sacrifice for our sins' mean? (Jesus' death on the cross (sacrifice) took the punishment (atoned) for all the bad things (sins) we and everyone else have ever done and ever will do.)

response

Love Hearts
(10 minutes)

It takes a while even to begin to get our head round God's love for us – it's unlike any love we have ever experienced or ever will experience.

Explain that there will be a few minutes of silence in which to think about what God's love might mean. Hand out a Love Heart to each young person in the group, making sure that they don't eat them until the end of the meditation. Play some quiet music if appropriate and read the meditation below. Have a short period of silence to give the young people some time to think and then end either with the prayer below or a prayer of your own choosing.

God loves you more than anyone else
ever has, ever will, ever can.
God's love is perfect;
never shouting, never ending, never leaving.
God's love will never change
no matter what you say,
no matter what you do,
no matter where you are.
God's love is Jesus;
in his life, in his death, in his return.

Dear God,
Thank you that you love each of us
        more than we can understand.
Thank you that you sent Jesus
        as a sign of just how much you love us.
Help us to respond to your love
        and to share it with others.
Amen.

EXTRAS and inserts

- Divide the young people into groups and play one of the love songs. Award a point to the first group to guess the song. Play the remaining songs, stopping at the end of each one. When you have listened to all the tracks, give a prize to the group with the most points.

- Divide the young people into groups and give each group a fruit or vegetable. Give them 5 minutes to come up with an ode to their fruit/vegetable. Encourage them to be as creative and slushy as they can! Get groups to perform their poems to each other.

- After making sure that none of the group is allergic to any of the ingredients, give everyone a biscuit. While they eat them, get the young people to talk about when and where the image of a heart is used.

consequences
GOD HAS PAID THE PRICE FOR OUR SIN

SESSION AIM.........	**To understand that our sin has consequences but Jesus took those consequences upon himself by dying on the cross**
EPISODE.............	Itchy and Scratchy: The Movie (season 4, episode 6)
CLIP................	Begin the clip just after Homer says, 'And this time I'll make it stick' (time code: 12:09) and end it after Homer tears up Bart's movie ticket (Duration: 3:25)
SYNOPSIS............	Bart makes a huge mistake when he puts Maggie's life in danger while he is supposed to be looking after her. Homer punishes him by not allowing him to go and see the new Itchy and Scratchy movie
KEY QUOTE...........	**Homer:** All right, Boy. This calls for the biggest punishment I ever handed down, and this time it's gonna stick.
BIBLE FOCUS........	'For the wages of sin is death, but the gift of God is eternal life in Christ Jesus our Lord.' (Romans 6.23)
RESOURCES..........	*Season 4 DVD 2, paper, pens, Bibles, bowl, 1p coins*
EXTRAS AND INSERTS	*Sets of dominoes (one set for each small group)*

- Fill a glass bowl with water – for a more visual effect, colour the water, using black-currant juice or a similar cordial (don't use a food dye as it will stain the skin!). Keep the water somewhere out of sight until you need it during the final activity.
- For Extras and inserts: prepare a list of 'crimes'.

Consequences
(10 minutes)

Begin by playing a game of consequences with the group. Give each person a piece of paper and say that without telling anyone else, they are to write down on the top of their paper the name of another person in the room. Once they have done this, they are to fold over the very top of the paper so the name can't be seen, and pass it to the person on their left. The next person then writes the next thing that you will read out, folds over the paper, and passes it on. The game continues until you've completed the items below.

- The name of a celebrity
- A wrong or stupid action
- A remark made by the celebrity

- What the first person said
- A consequence

At the end, get each group member to unfold the paper they are holding and read out the story that has been compiled as follows:

[Name of person in the room] met [name of celebrity], whereupon [wrong or silly action]. At this, the celebrity said ... and was told ... As a result ...

When all the stories have been read out, explain that today's session is about the consequences of the things we do wrong.

FOCUS
on simpsons

Itchy and Scratchy: The Movie

(25 minutes)
Watch the episode, or the clip if time is limited, in which we see Homer realizing that he has to punish Bart for what he did wrong. Get the group to think about the following questions:

- Why did Marge think they needed to punish Bart? (So he'd change his ways and learn that he mustn't behave badly.)
- What finally made Homer take the issue seriously? (Bart put Maggie's life in danger.)
- Do you think the punishment that Homer gave was fair?
- Did the punishment work? (Yes – Bart ended up as Chief Justice.)

FOCUS
on bible passage

Pay the price

(10 minutes)
Punishment is an uncomfortable word – being punished is not something any of us enjoys. However, just like Bart, we all come to realize that our actions have consequences, and the bad things we do will usually result in some sort of punishment. Paul talks about this in his letter to the church in Rome.

Get the group to look up Romans 6.23 and discuss the following questions:

- What does this verse say is the punishment for the bad things we do? (Death!) Emphasize that when Paul talks about death, he means complete separation from God at the end of our lives, rather than being killed.)
- *But* what does Romans 6.23 say God gave us instead? (Eternal life.)
- Why don't we have to pay the price for all the bad things we've done? Look at the end of the verse for a clue. (Jesus' death on the cross paid the price, once and for all, for all the bad things we, and everyone else, have done, and will do.)
- What do we have to do for God to forgive us? (All we have to do is be truly sorry for what we've done and ask God to forgive us.)

PRAYER
response

Forgiven

(10 minutes)
Everyone has done things that they know are wrong – we have all sinned. Yet Jesus' death on the cross means that we don't have to take the punishment – we can be forgiven by a God whose love is never ending.

Place the bowl of water in the middle of the circle and hand everyone a 1p coin. In a short time of quiet get the group to think about one thing they've done wrong (possibly recently, possibly some time ago) for which they want to say sorry to God.

Emphasize that they are not going to have to tell anyone else what it is. Once they've thought of something, tell them to come into the middle of the circle and place their 1p in the bowl of water as a sign that they are asking God to forgive them. (As always, make it clear that this is an optional activity.)

When everyone has had the opportunity to place their 1p in the bowl, close with a prayer of your choosing or use the prayer below.

Dear God,
Forgive us for these things we've thought about now.
Thank you that Jesus paid the price for all our sins.
Help us to be more like him as we live our lives.
Amen.

EXTRAS and inserts

- Divide the group into small groups of two to five, and give each group a set of dominoes. Explain that consequences are often like dominoes – once the first one goes, nothing can stop it knocking down the next and so on. Give the groups two minutes to line up as many dominoes as they can. Once the two minutes are up, see which group's line has the highest number dominoes.
- Divide the group into pairs and give each pair a 'crime' (you could include 'crimes' such as not tidying their bedroom, breaking a school window, murder, speeding in a car or cheating in a test). Get each pair to come up with what they think would be an appropriate consequence. How would they punish someone who had done this particular thing?

Temptation, Temptation, Temptation TEMPTATION

SESSION AIM.......... **To think about how to deal with temptations when they arise**

EPISODE............... Whacking Day (season 4, episode 20)

CLIP.................. Start the clip just after Mr Skinner laughs into the microphone (time code: 1:38) and end just after the tractor laughs at Bart for being expelled (Duration: 4:47)

SYNOPSIS............. Bart gets expelled from his school for embarrassing his head teacher, Mr Skinner, during an important school inspection

KEY QUOTES.......... **Tractor:** Come on, Bart, ride me.
Bart: I'd better not.
Tractor: Chicken!!!!!
Homer: Inside every man is a struggle between Good and Evil, which cannot be resolved.

BIBLE FOCUS......... 'No temptation has seized you except what is common to man. And God is faithful; he will not let you be tempted beyond what you can bear. But when you are tempted, he will also provide a way out so that you can stand up under it.' (1 Corinthians 10.13)

RESOURCES........... *Season 4 DVD 4, doughnuts, 'DO NOT TOUCH' sign, paper, pens, Bibles, playdough, A6 maps*

- Put out a plate of doughnuts (or other cakes enjoyed by your group) somewhere near where the young people enter, with a sign saying, 'DO NOT TOUCH'.
- Cut up photocopies of a map (it doesn't matter what it's a map of) into A6-sized sheets (A6 is a quarter of an A4 sheet). Do enough to give one to each young person.

Mmmmmm, doughnuts!
(15 minutes)
As the group arrive, leave the plate of doughnuts unattended and appear not to notice them. Make sure there are times when the young people are alone with the doughnuts. When you start, bring the plate into the middle of the group and ask:
- Who ate one of the doughnuts?
- Who really wanted to eat one?
- Why did/didn't they take one?

Introduce the theme and give each person a doughnut. While they are finishing their doughnuts, give each person a piece of playdough. Get everyone to make a model, or representation, of something that people might be tempted by (emphasize that this doesn't have to be a temptation that they themselves endure). When they are ready, get the group to try to guess what each model represents.

on simpsons

Whacking Day

(25 minutes)

Watch the episode in which Bart is tempted to ride the tractor, or the clip if time is limited, and then get the group to think about the following questions:

- What was Bart tempted to do? (He was tempted to ride the tractor.)
- Did he know that this would get him into trouble? (Yes!)
- Why did he end up doing it? (We all get tempted to do things we know are wrong – unfortunately these often seem fun. They're just not good for us in the long run. Often, we're weak and give in.)
- What happened to Bart as a result? (He ruined the school inspection and got expelled.)

on Bible passage

Be strong

(10 minutes)

Get the young people to look up 1 Corinthians 10.13. This is one of the things Paul wrote about temptation. As a group, think about the following questions:

- Does the verse say that Christians won't ever be tempted? (No!)
- What does it say that God will do when we're tempted? (When we're tempted, God will help us out.)
- What does the verse say about how God will do this? (God won't remove the temptations or make it so that we're never tempted. He will help us out. But this verse doesn't say how. We need to be looking for ways that will allow us to move away from whatever is tempting us.)

response

Lead us not . . .

(5 minutes)

Ask the group where they might have heard the line, 'Lead us not into temptation, but deliver us from evil.' Explain that when Christians pray these words in the Lord's Prayer, they are asking God to show them the route or path to follow to avoid the things that tempt them.

Give each person one of the A6 maps. Tell them to write a prayer on the back of their map asking God to guide them away from the thing(s) that tempt them, and to show them the way to go when they are tempted. Emphasize that this is a private activity – they won't have to show their prayer to anyone else.

Once everyone has had time to write their prayer, finish the activity with a closing prayer, either this one or a prayer of your own.

> Dear God,
> Lead us not into temptation.
> Show us how to avoid the things that tempt us.
> Give us ways to escape when we feel tempted.
> Deliver us from evil.
> Amen.

and inserts

- Divide the young people into pairs. Get them to come up with a mime (*no speaking!*) that shows someone being tempted. When they're ready, they can perform their mimes to the rest of the group, who will try to guess what the temptation is.

Not just stone
WHAT IS CHURCH?

SESSION AIM........	**To think about what church is and to understand that it's not just about a building**
EPISODE............	Homer the Heretic (season 4, episode 3)
CLIP...............	Start the clip from just after Marge shouts, 'No. What? What would help?' (time code: 6:35) and end it just after Homer's dream encounter with God (Duration: 3:29)
SYNOPSIS...........	Homer, in a dream, gets permission from God to skip church, much to Marge's dismay
KEY QUOTES.........	**Homer:** What's the big deal about going to some building every Sunday – I mean, isn't God everywhere?
	Marge: He doesn't mean to be sacrilegious, Lord, he just likes to sleep in on Sundays!
BIBLE FOCUS........	'For where two or three come together in my name, there am I with them.' (Matthew 18.20)
RESOURCES..........	*Season 4 DVD 1, Bibles, pictures of your church*
EXTRAS AND INSERTS	*pens and paper, Lego bricks*

● Print out enough pictures of your church to give one to each person.

True?
(10 minutes)
Begin the session with a 'True or False?' quiz. Read each of the statements below and ask whether the statement is true or false. Tell the young people to stand up if they think it's true, and to remain sitting if they think it's false. If you have enough space, and a more physical group, they can race to opposite ends of the room to answer 'true' or 'false'. Everyone with the correct answer gets a point. The overall winner is the person or team with the most points.

True or false?
1   The first church was built by the Romans. (False)
2   You have to go to church to be a Christian. (False)
3   A church *must* have pews. (False)
4   Our word 'church' comes from a Greek word that means, literally, 'a calling out of'. (True)

5   Peter was the only disciple to preach a sermon from a pulpit in a church. (False)
6   Going to church is an important part of being a Christian. (True)
7   You have to have at least 20 people before you count as a church. (False)
8   The churches Paul wrote letters to were based in people's houses. (True)
9   A vicar is the name of a person in charge of a particular type of church. (True)
10   It's against the law to build any new churches – we have to use old ones only.
     (False)

Homer the Heretic

(25 minutes)

Watch the episode in which we see Homer deciding not to go to church. If time is limited, watch the clip listed above. Get the group to think about the following questions:

- Why did Homer decide not to go to church? (Because he had more fun at home, he didn't see the point and it was boring.)
- Do you agree?
- Why did Marge want Homer to go to church? (She thought God would be angry if he didn't.)

Churchy

(15 minutes)

Explain that in fact both Homer and Marge had got it wrong. Out of the 115 times that the word 'church' is used in the New Testament part of the Bible, the word never refers to a building. Get the group to look up Matthew 18.17, 19 and 20, where Jesus is giving advice about what to do when we've been treated badly by another Christian. Discuss the following questions:

- These verses give a clue to the real meaning of 'church'. What do you think it might be? (In these verses 'church' refers to the people who are followers of Jesus. Church does also mean a building, of course, but that came later, and started as a short way of saying, 'the building where the church meets'.
- Why is being a member of a church an important part of being a Christian? (It's helpful to meet with other Christians to encourage each other and to pray and worship together. It's also a good way of learning from each other.)

Here's the church, here's the steeple

(5 minutes)

Give each young person a picture of your church and ask them to spend a few moments writing a prayer for their church on the back of the picture. Encourage them to think about praying for the people of the church, such as the clergy, and people they know who help in the church, or who are unwell, and for events and activities that the church runs.

Close with a prayer – you can use the prayer below or one of your own. Get the group to take home their prayers and ask them to continue to pray for their church throughout the week.

Dear God,
Thank you that wherever people meet in your name
   you are there with them.
We pray for our church.
We pray for all the people who go each week.
We ask that church will be a place
   where everyone can feel loved and welcomed.
Amen.

EXTRAS and inserts

- Give each person a piece of paper and a pen and say they have one minute to draw a 'church' – don't give them any more information and tell them not to discuss what they are drawing or copy from someone else. After the minute is up, go round looking at the group's sketches and getting each person to pick out the features of their drawing.

- Part of the role of church is to support its members in whatever they are going through. Get the young people to spend a few minutes writing a short note of encouragement to someone they know in the church who is having a tough time.

- Divide the young people into groups and get them to nominate a group leader. Give each group some Lego bricks. Gather together the group leaders and explain that their job is to get the rest of their group to use the bricks to build a model of a church. But, they are not allowed to tell the group what it is they are building, nor are they allowed to describe any of the parts of a church – they can only say where bricks should be placed. Set a time limit and see which group has built the best church.

Beautiful or wot! SELF-IMAGE

SESSION AIM . . . . **To think about how members of the group feel about the way they look and to see what God has to say on the subject**

EPISODE . . . . Lisa the Beauty Queen (season 4, episode 4)

CLIP . . . . Begin the clip just after Bart goes into the spook house (time code: 3:11) and end after Barney says, 'A guy like me can really clean up.' (Duration: 3:34)

SYNOPSIS . . . . Lisa competes in the 'Little Miss Springfield' competition and through a series of unlikely events, ends up winning. Her new role, however, is not as glamorous as she'd hoped

KEY QUOTES . . . . **Lisa:** Oh, my God! I'm ugly!
Lisa: But the point is, you wanted me to feel better about myself, and I do.

BIBLE FOCUS . . . . 'I praise you because I am fearfully and wonderfully made;
your works are wonderful,
I know that full well.' (Psalm 139.14)

RESOURCES . . . . *Season 4 DVD 1, aluminium foil, pens, paper, Bibles, card, pencils, felt-tip pens, quiet music*

EXTRAS AND INSERTS *Newspapers and magazines, scissors, glue, paper, ink-pads, pieces of paper, wet wipes*

- Prepare enough pieces of tin foil to give one to each member of the group. The pieces each need to be about 50 cm square.
- Cut A4 sheets into quarters (to make into A6 sheets), enough to give one to each member of the group.

Aluminium beauty
(15 minutes)
To start the session, give each member of the group a piece of tinfoil and say that they are to take an impression of their face. Demonstrate by pressing the tinfoil over your face, pressing it into the contours of your nose, eyes, etc. to get the best possible mould. If you wear glasses, it's easier to take them off first!

Once everyone has a tinfoil impression of their face, get the group to judge how true to life the likenesses are.

Give each person a piece of paper and, using the impressions they've made, ask the young people to look at themselves and write down two things about their face that they like, and one thing that they think doesn't look so good, or looks a bit funny, or they would like to change. Emphasize that this is a private activity and they don't have to show anyone else what they've written. (If you are running a shortened session, you might want to skip this part.)

Lisa the Beauty Queen
(25 minutes)

Watch the episode in which Lisa enters a beauty contest, or the clip if your time is limited, and then talk about the following questions:

- Why did Homer enter Lisa into a beauty contest? (He wanted to prove to her that she wasn't ugly.)
- How did her family change her to make her look 'prettier'? (New outfit, new haircut.)
- Was she happy with her new look? (Yes – it made her popular – people looked up to her.)
- What did Lisa learn? (That she could feel better about herself by standing up for what she believed in, rather than by looking like someone she wasn't.)

Wonderful
(10 minutes)

All of us have things about the way we look that we don't like. However, the Bible has something to say about how we should feel about ourselves. Get the group to look up Psalm 139.14.

- What does this verse tells us? (God has made each one of us and he thinks we are amazing.)
- How can we apply what we read in this verse to how we feel about the way we look? (We can keep on reminding ourselves that we are perfect examples of God's craftsmanship – if he made us, then he must want us to look exactly the way we do look. We are each truly beautiful in God's eyes.)
- Does the group think it's easy to believe and feel this?

Beautiful
(5 minutes)

Give each person the A6 piece of card and put out some pens, pencils and felt-tip pens. Tell the young people to draw a simple picture of themselves on the card, and copy out today's verse below it. As they are drawing and writing, play some quiet music.

Encourage the young people to take their cards home and put them up somewhere where they will see them every day, for example, on a mirror or door as a reminder of what God thinks about the way they look.

Close with a prayer of your choosing or use the prayer below.

Dear God,
Thank you for making us just the way we are.
Help me to remember that we are just as you intended,
fearfully and wonderfully made.
Amen.

 **and inserts**

- Gather together a selection of magazines and newspapers (make sure they don't have content you wouldn't want your young people reading!). Give them out, along with paper, scissors and glue. Get each person to make a collage of what they think a 'beautiful' person looks like by sticking together parts from different pictures in the magazines and newspapers. They might choose the eyes of one person, the ears of another and the mouth of a third celebrity, or they might choose one celebrity's torso, another's arms and the head of a third.

- Give the young people the ink-pads and paper. Tell them to make their fingerprints on their paper and then compare their prints with those of others in the group. Look at the differences – each one is unique. Yet God knows them all! Make sure you have some wet wipes on hand for inky fingers!

FRIENDSHIP

SESSION AIM........ **To consider the importance of friends**

EPISODE............ Mr Plow (season 4, episode 9)

CLIP.............. Start the clip just after Barney gets presented with the keys to the city (time code: 16:38) and continue to the end of the episode (Duration: 4:26)

SYNOPSIS........... Best friends Homer and Barney become business competitors. But a dangerous trick teaches Homer a valuable lesson

KEY QUOTE......... **Homer:** When two best friends work together, not even God himself can stop them.

BIBLE FOCUS........ 'Two are better than one, because they have a good return for their work: If one falls down, his friend can help him up. But pity the man who falls and has no one to help him up! Also, if two lie down together, they will keep warm. But how can one keep warm alone? Though one may be overpowered, two can defend themselves. A cord of three strands is not quickly broken.' (Ecclesiastes 4.9-12)

RESOURCES......... *Season 4 DVD 2, Post-it notes, pens, paper, scissors, Bibles*

EXTRAS AND INSERTS *Gingerbread figures, something to decorate them with, paper, pens or pencils, materials to make friendship bracelets*

- Write one of the following names on Post-it notes: Dennis the Menace, Gnasher, Harry Potter, Ron, Scooby Doo, Scrappy Doo, Timon, Pumba, Chandler, Joey, Bart, Milhouse, Homer, Barney. (Add more names if your group is larger. One Post-it note for each group member.)
- For Extras and inserts: Find out how to make friendship bracelets – typing, 'How to make a friendship bracelet' into Google comes up with several explanations.

Just good friends
(15 minutes)
Introduce the theme, and stick one of the Post-it notes to each person's forehead (so that they cannot read it themselves!). Each person has to go round and find out the name of the character on their Post-it note by asking other members of the group questions to which the answer can only be yes or no. Once they find out who they are, they need to find their 'mate'.

Use these examples of friendship to discuss with the group why it's good to have friends – what are the benefits? Are there any negative aspects – are friends always kind and helpful? When is it essential to have friends? When can we do without them?

Mr Plow

(25 minutes)

Watch the episode, or the clip if time is limited, and then think about the following questions:

- What did Barney do to Homer? (He stole Homer's idea and started a rival snow-ploughing business.)
- How did Homer feel? (He felt let down by Barney.)
- What did Homer do in response? (He called Barney and sent him up to plough Widow's Peaks, stealing his customers while he was busy.)
- What lesson did Homer learn? (He learned that friends should work together and help each other rather than competing and stabbing each other in the back.)

M8Z R GR8

(10 minutes)

The Bible has a very clear message about friends. One example of the Bible's teaching can be found in the book of Ecclesiastes. Get the group to look up Ecclesiastes 4.9-12 and talk through the following questions:

- What do these verses say are the benefits of having friends? (A friend will help you when you're in trouble or have a problem; a friend supports you in the bad and the good times.)
- How might these ideas be explained using modern examples – when do our friends help us?

Pray for 'em

(10 minutes)

Show the group how to use A4 paper and scissors to make a paper concertina of little figures (just like you used to make in infant school!). On each of the figures get them to write the name of one of their friends.

When everyone has finished, say a short prayer. You can use the prayer below or come up with your own. Give an opportunity for each person to say the names of the people they've written on their paper figures. Ask the young people to take their figures home so that they can continue to pray for their friends during the week.

Dear God,
Thank you for our friends.
Thank you for the times
    when our friends help us up
    when we've fallen down.
Help us to be good friends to others,
    always looking for ways to support them.
We particularly thank you for . . .
    [include the names written by the young people].
Thank you for the ways they help us.
Amen.

- Get the young people to decorate a gingerbread person to look like one of their friends. See if the rest of the group can guess who it is.
- Get the young people to make a friendship bracelet — if suitable, talk about who they might give it to as a sign of their friendship.
- Have each member of the group write their name on a piece of paper. Collect them in, jumble them up and give them out again, making sure no one gets their own paper! Explain that in the coming week they are going to be a 'mate' to the person on their piece of paper. They should try to do something kind for that person in the next seven days. It can be absolutely anything, but should be anonymous. (No one has to say who their 'mate' is.)

PART TWO

Going deeper

Build 'em up! ENCOURAGING OTHERS WITH OUR WORDS

SESSION AIM......... **To think about how our words can encourage those around us**

EPISODE.............. A Streetcar Named Marge (season 4, episode 2)

CLIP................. Watch the episode from the beginning up to the point at which Homer says, 'That's OK, we're none of us perfect.' (Duration: 3:58)

SYNOPSIS............ Marge auditions for, and stars in, a musical version of *A Streetcar Named Desire*, but the rest of the Simpson family are not as encouraging as they might be

KEY QUOTES......... **Marge:** I spend all day alone with Maggie and sometimes it's like I don't even exist.

Marge: Why can't you be a little more supportive?

BIBLE FOCUS........ 'Therefore encourage one another and build each other up, just as in fact you are doing.' (1 Thessalonians 5.11)

RESOURCES........... *Season 4 DVD 1, Bibles, pens, large sheet of paper, newspapers, glue, scissors*

EXTRAS AND INSERTS *Sellotape (or safety pins), pens and pencils, sheets of paper (one for each member)*

- Gather together suitable newspapers for the final prayer activity.
- For Extras and inserts: write out the list of words that you'll be reading out.

Happy nice lovely
(10 minutes)
Ask the young people to get into pairs and give each pair a piece of paper and pen or pencil. The object of the game is to come up with positive words and compliments that no other pair has thought of. They have 2 minutes to write down as many complimentary words, such as 'nice, cool, great etc.', as they can. Encourage them to be as creative as possible.
After 2 minutes, ask the group to stop writing. The pairs take it in turns to call out their words and they get a point each time they are the only ones with a word. The pair with the most points wins!

A Streetcar named Marge

(*25 minutes*)

Tell the young people that during this session they'll be looking at how we can encourage others around us by our words. Bearing this in mind, watch the episode ' A Streetcar named Marge', or the clip if time is limited. Then ask the group to consider the following questions:

- How did Marge feel about the way her family reacted when she told them she was auditioning for a play? (She was upset that they didn't seem to care – they were more interested in watching the television programme than in what she was doing.)
- Did her family encourage her in what she was doing? (No – they didn't seem to care about anything other than their own interests and concerns.)
- Did the director encourage his actors? (No – his remarks were harsh and he made people feel small.)
- What could her family have said to Marge that might have encouraged her?
- How do we feel when people don't encourage us and don't praise us and tell us we're doing well?

Build 'em up

(*10 minutes*)

Ask the group to look up 1 Thessalonians 5.11 and think about the following questions:

- What does this verse tell us to do? (Encourage one another. It's important to use our words to make the people around us feel good about themselves. We must not put people down.)
- Why might this verse have been especially important in the first churches to whom Paul was writing? (Things were often very tough. Their numbers were small and the Christians were often misunderstood and persecuted by the people around them. Therefore it was important for them to look after each other and encourage each other.)
- How can we encourage those around us?

We need to help people when they're down and praise them when they do well.

Newspaper praise

(*10 minutes*)

Hand out pages from newspapers (being careful to check the contents first!), scissors and glue and place a large piece of paper in the middle of the group. Ask the young people to cut out words and phrases that are positive and encouraging and stick them on to the paper to make up a group collage. Encourage them to do this activity quietly.

At the end, draw the activities and discussions together with a prayer. You could use your own prayer or the prayer below.

Dear God,
Thank you for the gift of words.
Help us to use what we say to encourage those around us.
Help us to build people up
    rather than making them feel ignored and discouraged.
Amen.

EXTRAS and inserts

- If your group know each other reasonably well, tape or pin a sheet of paper to their backs and give everyone a pen. Tell them to go round and write nice things about the other members of the group on the pieces of paper on their backs. They could write characteristics that they like about the other person, or things that person is good at, or they have been impressed by. Ensure that everything that is being written is positive – make it clear before you start that this activity is to be taken seriously.

- Explain to the group that you are going to read out a word – and they will have to decide whether or not it's a complimentary word. Read out the words below and after each word, get the young people to split into two groups – one group that thinks the word could be used as a compliment and one that wouldn't be very happy if someone used this word to describe them. Tell them to keep their own score and at the end see who has got the most right. Words you could use are:

maleficent (bad)   reprehensible (bad)
illustrious (good)   reprobate (bad)
cordial (good)   abominable (bad)
genial (good)   prodigious (good)
depraved (bad)   atrocious (bad)
stupendous (good)

Is it 'cos I is young? YOUNG PEOPLE ARE PART OF GOD'S PLAN

SESSION AIM........	**To understand that God uses young people as part of his plan**
EPISODE............	The Front (season 4, episode 18)
CLIP...............	Start the clip just after Homer says to Marge in the living room, 'I don't know – I flunked Latin too' (time code: 4:01) and run it until Bart says, 'He let those guys use his cheque-book for a whole year.' (Duration: 2:20)
SYNOPSIS...........	Lisa and Bart write an Itchy and Scratchy cartoon but don't get taken seriously because of their age
KEY QUOTE..........	**Lisa:** Maybe he just doesn't take us seriously 'cos we're kids.
BIBLE FOCUS........	'Don't let anyone look down on you because you are young, but set an example for the believers in speech, in life, in love, in faith and in purity.' (1 Timothy 4.12)
RESOURCES..........	*Season 4 DVD 4, paper, pens, Bibles*
EXTRAS AND INSERTS	*A collection of newspapers, photographs of members of the group at different ages*

- Check that you know the ages at which the law allows young people to vote, buy alcohol, get married, drive, and so on. You can look this up at <www.met.police.uk/askthemet/456.htm>.
- For Extras and inserts: speak to parents and guardians of members of your group and get hold of photographs of members at different ages.

Too young, too old
(10 minutes)

Divide the young people into small groups and get each group to come up with two lists – one of things they are allowed to do now but won't be able to do when they're 'grown up', and another of things they would like to do but can't because they're too young. Encourage them to think about how old they have to be before they can legally buy alcohol, drive a car, get married, and so on. Once each group has come up with their two lists, call all the groups together to feed back their comments.

The Front
(25 minutes)

Watch the episode, or the clip if time is limited, in which we see Bart and Lisa not being taken seriously because they're young. Then think about the questions below:
- Why did Roger Mayers (the editor of *Itchy and Scratchy*) reject Lisa and Bart's script? (Because they were children.)

- What did they have to do to get their script noticed? (Put an adult's name on it.)
- Do the group have any examples of times when people haven't taken them seriously because they weren't adults?
- Why is it necessary to have *some* things, such as driving, that are restricted to certain ages?
- Look back at the lists the young people made during the first activity. Why are there some things you can only do when you're young?
- Why do people base their judgement of others on their age?

FOCUS
on Bible passage

Dear Timmy . . .

(10 minutes)

Get the group to look up 1 Timothy 4.12. Explain that this verse is part of a letter from St Paul to a young man named Timothy.

- Why did Paul write this verse to Timothy? (Timothy was a young man leading a church – we can guess that some were ignoring what he was saying because of his age.)
- What advice did Paul give that can help us today? (Paul told Timothy to keep doing what he was doing – living his life the way God had told him to. We can do the same. No matter how old we are, we can all live our lives the way God wants us to.)

PRAYER
response

A good example?

(*10 minutes*)

Timothy wouldn't have found it easy to follow Paul's advice; it isn't easy today. Setting an example of how to speak and live and relate to other people in the way God wants is hard. There are so many things to stop us. Ask the young people to spend a few moments thinking about areas of their lives where it's difficult to live God's way.

Have a time of quiet when the young people can pray, either out loud or in silence, asking God to help them to set an example to others.

Finish by praying for the group, either using the prayer below, or a prayer of your own.

> Dear God,
> Help us, like Timothy, to live lives
>   that set an example to those around us.
> Guide what we say.
> Guide how we live.
> Guide how we love.
>   making us more like you each day.
> Amen.

EXTRAS
and inserts

- Gather together a collection of newspapers, making sure that none contains any unsuitable material. Have the young people look through them and pick out stories about young people. Identify which stories show young people in a positive light and which are negative. Talk with the group about why they think there is usually more negative than positive news when young people are mentioned.
- Put up around the room the photographs of your group when they were young and have the group guess who is who and how old they were when the photographs were taken.

SESSION AIM.........	**To think about the impact of gossip on our relationships with others**
EPISODE.............	Marge in Chains (season 4, episode 21)
CLIP...............	Begin the clip just after Homer leaves the Kwik-E-Mart, having asked Apu to drop the charges (time code: 10:09) and end just after Maude says, 'Just wash your hands and get out.' (Duration: 1:13)
SYNOPSIS...........	In a state of near exhaustion, Marge accidentally shoplifts at the Kwik-E-Mart and gets sentenced to 30 days in the local prison
KEY QUOTE	**Maude Flanders:** From now on I'll use my gossip for good instead of evil.
BIBLE FOCUS........	'As a north wind brings rain, so a sly tongue brings angry looks.' (Proverbs 25.23)
	'A perverse man stirs up dissension, and a gossip separates close friends.' (Proverbs 16.28)
RESOURCES..........	*Season 4 DVD 4, Bibles, bowl of honey*
EXTRAS AND INSERTS	*A collection of newspapers, paper, glue, felt-tip pens, scissors*

●   Check that none of your group is allergic to honey!

Whispers . . . whispers
(5 minutes)

Begin by getting the group to play a game of Chinese whispers. Start by choosing the phrases or words yourself, using simple, true statements about members of the group, for example, 'John wears glasses.' Once they get the idea, ask members of the group to set the phrase. After a few rounds, talk about how mangled the phrases get as they are passed from person to person. Sometimes this happens in real life as we pass on gossip. This gossip can cause pain and hurt.

Marge in Chains
(*25 minutes*)

Watch the episode in which Marge gets herself into a sticky situation. If you don't have time to see the whole episode, watch the clip listed above. Ask:
●   What did people say about Marge behind her back? (She was a thief, she made gingerbread men with hair in them, she has webbed toes, she drinks too much, etc.)
●   Why were they gossiping about her? (It was something to talk about – it's interesting to talk about other people's failures and flaws.)

- What was the effect of their gossip? (People like Maude Flanders didn't trust her – they saw her differently.)
- What lessons does the group think Maude and others had learned by the end of the episode?

FOCUS
on bible passage

Troublemaking

(*10 minutes*)

Gossip can be very damaging to friendships – it can cause a lot of problems. Get the group to look up Proverbs 25.23 and 16.28. Explain that the book of Proverbs is a collection of wise sayings. If you have been using the New International Version, you might want to look up these verses in a version of the Bible that makes them slightly easier to understand.

- Does the group agree with what the writer says about gossip?
- How does gossip cause angry looks and separate close friends?
- How can we avoid being drawn into gossip?
- If we are tempted to gossip, what could we do instead?

PRAYER
response

Sweet like honey

(*5 minutes*)

Proverbs 16.24 says, 'Pleasant words are a honeycomb, sweet to the soul and healing to the bones.' Place a bowl of honey in the middle of the group. Play some quiet music in the background and encourage the group to pray a silent prayer asking God to help them use their words for good rather than for gossip. As a sign of this commitment, they should dip their finger in the bowl and taste some of the honey. Emphasize that they don't have to do this if they don't want to.

Finish the activity with a prayer – you can use the prayer below or one of your own.

Dear God,
Thank you for giving us the gift of speech.
Help us to use our words to encourage and
   help others
   rather than to gossip and hurt those around us.
Amen.

EXTRAS
and inserts

Extras and inserts

- The word THINK is a short way of reminding ourselves about gossip. Whenever we are tempted to pass something we know about one person on to someone else, we should ask ourselves whether it is:

True   **Helpful**   **Inspiring**   **Necessary**   **Kind**

If it's not, we shouldn't pass it on. Get the young people to cut out letters from the headlines of newspapers and stick them on to a piece of paper to spell the word 'THINK'. Tell them to design a border and decorate the letters while fixing the word and its meaning in their minds.

Sibling rivalry
BROTHERS AND SISTERS

SESSION AIM.........	**To think about how we treat our siblings**
EPISODE.............	Duffless (season 4, episode 16)
CLIP................	Begin the clip just after Selma voids Homer's driving licence (time code: 9:10) and end it when Lisa says, 'Hamster 2, Bart 0.' (Duration: 1:51)
SYNOPSIS............	When Bart ruins Lisa's science project, Lisa retaliates, trying to get back at him for what he did
KEY QUOTE	**Lisa:** I propose to answer the question, 'Is my brother dumber than a hamster?'
BIBLE FOCUS........	'This is the message you heard from the beginning: We should love one another. Do not be like Cain, who belonged to the evil one and murdered his brother. And why did he murder him? Because his own actions were evil and his brother's were righteous.' (1 John 3.11-12)
RESOURCES..........	Season 4 DVD 3, Bibles, pens, pebbles, paper, lining paper, scissors
EXTRAS AND INSERTS	Pictures of celebrity siblings, Blu-tack, paper, pencils

- Gather enough stones or pebbles to give one to each member of the group – they will need to be smooth enough to write on.
- Cut up the lining paper into long pieces (see opening activity). Do enough to give one to each small group.
- For Extras and inserts: use the Internet to download pictures of different celebrity siblings. You might include pictures of the following famous brothers and sisters: Bart and Lisa Simpson, Kylie and Dannii Minogue, David and Joanne Beckham, Serena and Venus Williams, and The Corrs. Number the pictures.

Pros and cons
(10 minutes)
Divide the group into smaller groups. Give each small group a piece of the lining paper and tell the young people to draw round one of their group. Inside the outline they have just drawn get them to write the good things about having a brother or sister. Around the outside of their drawing get them to write all the bad things. Give the group some time to write both lists before feeding back to the rest of the group.

If there are any only children in your group, tell them that Jesus said that other Christians are our brothers and sisters (Mark 3.35). So they can think about someone in their group or the church who they can't get on with.

FOCUS on simpsons

Duffless

(25 minutes)

Watch the episode, or the clip listed above if time is limited, in which we see another occasion when Bart and Lisa don't get on – Bart destroyed Lisa's science project so out of revenge, Lisa found a way to get back at him. Ask the group to think about the following questions:

- Why don't Bart and Lisa get on? (Sometimes brothers and sisters just don't! They might be too similar in personality, or living together might make them get on each other's nerves.)
- Do you think Bart and Lisa love each other?
- Do they show it? If not, why not?

FOCUS on Bible passage

Brotherly love

(10 minutes)

The Bible has many stories about siblings who don't get on – Cain and Abel, Joseph and his brothers. Even Jesus knew about bossy brothers. In John's Gospel we read, 'Even his own brothers did not believe in him' (John 7.5). And at one point they actually thought he had gone mad and set out to stop him preaching and healing (Mark 3.21, 32). John has an important message for us about how we should treat our brothers and sisters. Look up 1 John 3.11

- What does this verse say about how we should treat our siblings (or other Christians)? (We need to love them!)
- What sorts of things could we do to love our brothers and sisters?

PRAYER response

Stony silence

(10 minutes)

It's not easy – brothers and sisters annoy us almost as much as we annoy them. Getting on with them is just something each one of us has to work on. One of the things that we can all do is pray for them. Hand each member of the group a pebble. On their pebble, get them to write the names of their siblings (or Christian brothers and sisters). Go round the group and get each member to pray for the people they've written down. It doesn't have to be a long or complicated prayer – 'Dear God, help me to get along wit ... Amen' is all that's needed.

Get the group to take the stones home as a reminder to pray for their brothers and sisters, even when they really get on their nerves!

Close with a prayer – either one of your own or this one.

> Dear God,
> Thank you for our brothers and sisters
>   and for our friends who are our brothers and sisters
>   because they are Christians.
> Thank you for the times they help us out
>   and for the times when they share our jokes and our tears.
> Help us to get along with them
>   even when they are really annoying.
> Amen.

EXTRAS and inserts

- Put up around the room the pictures of celebrity siblings. Give the young people the chance to go round and try to match up the siblings based on the pictures – award extra points for any names they can remember!

first aid
PRAYING FOR THE SICK

SESSION AIM......... **To understand the importance of praying for those who are sick**

EPISODE............. Homer's Triple Bypass (season 4, episode 11)

CLIP............... Start the clip where Homer is playing with the droodel (spinning top) (timecode 11:31) and continue until the scene ends and it fades to black (Duration: 3:00)

SYNOPSIS........... Homer's unhealthy lifestyle finally catches up with him when he has a heart attack

KEY QUOTES......... **Moe:** Now let's have a minute of silent prayer for our good friend, Homer Simpson.
Barney: How long has it been?
Moe: Six seconds.
Barney: Do we have to start over?
Moe: Hell, no.

BIBLE FOCUS........ 'Is any one of you sick? He should call the elders of the church to pray over him and anoint him with oil in the name of the Lord.' (James 5.14)

RESOURCES.......... *Season 4 DVD 3, bandages, Bibles, plasters, paper, pens, sheet of paper*

EXTRAS AND INSERTS *Unopened toilet rolls or strips of material (for bandages)*

- People who are ill might be a very sensitive topic for some members of your group – if you know that family members or friends of members of your group are ill, make sure you pay particular attention to how they are doing during this session.
- For Extras and inserts: find out if your church has a regular list of people who are sick or unwell, and for whom prayers are asked. Copy out this list.

Slings a' plenty
(10 minutes)
To introduce the theme of the session, begin by teaching the group how to put on an arm-sling using a triangular bandage. If you don't know how to do one yourself, get a local member of the St John Ambulance or the Red Cross to show you. Hand out bandages and let the young people work in pairs to produce the perfect sling.

Homer's Triple Bypass
(25 minutes)
Watch the episode in which Homer needs a heart bypass. If time is limited, watch the clip. Get the group to think about the following questions:

- When Homer found out he was ill, what were some of the things he did? (He gave advice to Bart and Lisa, looked after Marge, had a beer and prayed.)
- How did Homer's friends respond when they found out he was ill? (They bought him presents and they prayed for him.)

FOCUS on Bible passage

Take action

(10 minutes)

At times, all of us know people who are unwell or who are hurt or injured, and it can be upsetting to think that there is very little we can do to help them. However, the Bible says there is something we can do. Get the group to have a look at James 5.14.

- What does this verse say we should do if people are ill? (Pray for them and anoint them with oil – although anointing with oil is probably best left to vicars!)
- What does the verse say God will do when we pray? (It doesn't say – we can't know or guess what God will do! We have to pray and leave the rest to God. We should pray, believing that God can help. He might help by making the person calmer or making them better more quickly, or even help in ways that we don't see. But we can be certain that if we pray for someone who is unwell, God always hears our prayers and will be with that person.)

PRAYER response

Put a plaster on it!

(10 minutes)

Finish the session by giving the group a chance to pray for people they know who are injured or unwell, mentally or physically. Put down a sheet of paper in the middle of the group and give each person a sticking plaster and a pen. They should write the name of the person they want to pray for on the plaster and then stick their plaster on the paper. Explain that they can pray for more than one person if they wish.

Finish with a short closing prayer. Use the prayer below or make up your own.

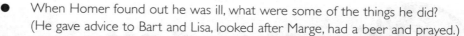

Dear God,
Please be with those people we know
    who are not well, or are injured.
Comfort them and let them know that you are with them.
Help those who care for them
    and give them the skills they need to do their jobs.
Amen.

EXTRAS and inserts

- Hand out strips of material or unopened rolls of toilet paper and give the group 5 minutes to work in pairs to bandage up their partner as completely as they can!
- Get the group to look through the list of sick people your church is praying for – are there names that the young people recognize? Divide the names up among the young people and get them to pray for the people on their list throughout the coming week.

SESSION AIM......... **To start to think about the idea of the second coming – that is, the return of Jesus**

EPISODE............. Kamp Krusty (season 4, episode 1)

CLIP................ Start the clip just after Bart and Lisa have left to go to camp and the parents celebrate (timecode: 9:36), ending it after Jimbo says, 'Looks like we got ourselves a troublemaker.' (Duration: 1:00)

SYNOPSIS............ Bart and Lisa go off to Kamp Krusty for the summer holiday, but the camp turns out to be not quite what Bart and Lisa were expecting as they anxiously await the return of their hero

KEY QUOTES.......... **Bart:** When do we get to see Krusty?
Mr Black: Uuh, he'll be along eventually. In the meantime, our counsellors Dolph, Jimbo and Kearney will be happy to handle any problems you might have.

BIBLE FOCUS .... 'Do not let your hearts be troubled. Trust in God; trust also in me. In my Father's house are many rooms; if it were not so, I would have told you. I am going there to prepare a place for you. And if I go and prepare a place for you, I will come back and take you to be with me that you also may be where I am.' (John 14.1-3)

RESOURCES........... *Season 4 DVD 1, paper, pens, Bibles*

EXTRAS AND INSERTS *Art materials (paints, pens, scraps of fabric, etc. to make collages), scissors, glue*

- Make sure you have a piece of paper for every member of the group.

Looking forward to ...
(10 minutes)
Start by getting everyone to think of one thing in the near future that they are really looking forward to. Get them to try to think of something interesting – something that might be a little obscure, or that's a specific event, rather than 'football'. Have them write their event down on a piece of paper, collect them in and jumble them up. Read out each piece one by one and get the group to guess who is looking forward to what.

Kamp Krusty
(25 minutes)
Watch the episode in which Bart and Lisa desperately await the return of their hero. If time is limited, watch the clip suggested above. Get the group to think about the following questions:
- What made the members of Kamp Krusty so sure Krusty was coming back? (Krusty had said he would be there in the adverts that Bart and Lisa had seen on television promoting the camp. Then, when they arrived at camp, they'd seen a video of Krusty promising that he would be there soon.)

- How do you think they felt about the idea that Krusty was coming back to see them soon? (They were excited about it – even though the rest of the camp was pretty awful, the idea that their hero was going to come back gave them hope.) Did they know when Krusty would return? (No – they had no idea when.)
- What did they do in the meantime? (They carried on with the activities at the camp, hoping for Krusty's return.)

Coming soon

(10 minutes)

We all have things we're looking forward to, but the great event that Christians are waiting for is the return of Jesus.

Have the group look up John 14.1-3. Talk through the following questions:
- What makes Christians so sure that Jesus is coming back? (He promised he would return.)
- What did Jesus go away to do? (Prepare a place for us in heaven.)
- How do Christians feel about his return? (They are looking forward to it.)
- Can the group think of things we should be doing while we await his return?

Reassure the group that if any of this sounds difficult to get their heads round, they are not alone. There's a lot we don't know – for example, Jesus didn't say when he would return – but we do know we need to be ready!

Excited expectations

(10 minutes)

Finish the session by asking each person to choose something they are doing in the future that they would like to pray about. Each time a member of the group has chosen something, ask for a volunteer to pray for that person (you might want to write down who is praying for what). When everyone has chosen and has someone else to pray for them, go round the circle and get each person to pray – their prayer doesn't need to be complicated. It can be as simple as, 'Dear God, please help Joe at his football match next week. Amen.' End with a prayer of your own choosing or use this one.

Dear God,
Thank you that you are with us
wherever we are,
whatever we are doing.
Help us in the things we have prayed for
as we wait for your return.
Amen.

- Get the group to shut their eyes as you read John's description of heaven from Revelation 21. Ask what they thought about and imagined and how they felt as they listened. Give them time and space to use the collage materials to make a picture in response to what they heard.
- Divide the young people into groups and ask them to imagine that an important guest is coming to stay for the weekend. What will they need to do in order to get ready? Suppose they found out that the guest was Jesus. Would they do anything differently? When they are ready, feed back to the whole group.